This study guide was created to help you process your thoughts, write down important verses, allow you to think about how the verses relate to your life for retention, and write short notes for each chapter as you are studying the bible. Enjoy the journey!

-R. Parker

Genesis

Chapter 1

MY INTERPRETATION OF VERSES...

VERSES THAT STOOD OUT TO ME

NOTES

HOW THIS CHAPTER RELATES TO MY LIFE

Genesis

Chapter 2

MY INTERPRETATION OF VERSES...

VERSES THAT STOOD OUT TO ME

NOTES

HOW THIS CHAPTER RELATES TO MY LIFE

Genesis

Chapter 3

MY INTERPRETATION OF VERSES...

VERSES THAT STOOD OUT TO ME

NOTES

HOW THIS CHAPTER RELATES TO MY LIFE

Genesis

Chapter 4

MY INTERPRETATION OF VERSES...

VERSES THAT STOOD OUT TO ME

NOTES

HOW THIS CHAPTER RELATES TO MY LIFE

Genesis

Chapter 5

MY INTERPRETATION OF VERSES...

VERSES THAT STOOD OUT TO ME

NOTES

HOW THIS CHAPTER RELATES TO MY LIFE

Genesis

Chapter 6

MY INTERPRETATION OF VERSES...

VERSES THAT STOOD OUT TO ME

NOTES

HOW THIS CHAPTER RELATES TO MY LIFE

Genesis

Chapter 7

MY INTERPRETATION OF VERSES...

VERSES THAT STOOD OUT TO ME

NOTES

HOW THIS CHAPTER RELATES TO MY LIFE

Genesis

Chapter 8

MY INTERPRETATION OF VERSES...

VERSES THAT STOOD OUT TO ME

NOTES

HOW THIS CHAPTER RELATES TO MY LIFE

Genesis

Chapter 9

MY INTERPRETATION OF VERSES...

VERSES THAT STOOD OUT TO ME

NOTES

HOW THIS CHAPTER RELATES TO MY LIFE

Genesis

Chapter 10

MY INTERPRETATION OF VERSES...

VERSES THAT STOOD OUT TO ME

NOTES

HOW THIS CHAPTER RELATES TO MY LIFE

Genesis

Chapter 11

MY INTERPRETATION OF VERSES...

VERSES THAT STOOD OUT TO ME

NOTES

HOW THIS CHAPTER RELATES TO MY LIFE

Genesis

Chapter 12

MY INTERPRETATION OF VERSES...

VERSES THAT STOOD OUT TO ME

NOTES

HOW THIS CHAPTER RELATES TO MY LIFE

Genesis

Chapter 13

MY INTERPRETATION OF VERSES...

VERSES THAT STOOD OUT TO ME

NOTES

HOW THIS CHAPTER RELATES TO MY LIFE

Genesis

Chapter 14

MY INTERPRETATION OF VERSES...

VERSES THAT STOOD OUT TO ME

NOTES

HOW THIS CHAPTER RELATES TO MY LIFE

Genesis

Chapter 15

MY INTERPRETATION OF VERSES...

VERSES THAT STOOD OUT TO ME

NOTES

HOW THIS CHAPTER RELATES TO MY LIFE

Genesis

Chapter 16

MY INTERPRETATION OF VERSES...

VERSES THAT STOOD OUT TO ME

NOTES

HOW THIS CHAPTER RELATES TO MY LIFE

Genesis

Chapter 17

MY INTERPRETATION OF VERSES...

VERSES THAT STOOD OUT TO ME

NOTES

HOW THIS CHAPTER RELATES TO MY LIFE

Genesis

Chapter 18

MY INTERPRETATION OF VERSES...

VERSES THAT STOOD OUT TO ME

NOTES

HOW THIS CHAPTER RELATES TO MY LIFE

Genesis

Chapter 19

MY INTERPRETATION OF VERSES...

VERSES THAT STOOD OUT TO ME

NOTES

HOW THIS CHAPTER RELATES TO MY LIFE

Genesis

Chapter 20

MY INTERPRETATION OF VERSES...

VERSES THAT STOOD OUT TO ME

NOTES

HOW THIS CHAPTER RELATES TO MY LIFE

Genesis

Chapter 21

MY INTERPRETATION OF VERSES...

VERSES THAT STOOD OUT TO ME

NOTES

HOW THIS CHAPTER RELATES TO MY LIFE

Genesis

Chapter 22

MY INTERPRETATION OF VERSES...

VERSES THAT STOOD OUT TO ME

NOTES

HOW THIS CHAPTER RELATES TO MY LIFE

Genesis

Chapter 23

MY INTERPRETATION OF VERSES...

VERSES THAT STOOD OUT TO ME

NOTES

HOW THIS CHAPTER RELATES TO MY LIFE

Genesis

Chapter 24

MY INTERPRETATION OF VERSES...

VERSES THAT STOOD OUT TO ME

HOW THIS CHAPTER RELATES TO MY LIFE

NOTES

Genesis

Chapter 25

MY INTERPRETATION OF VERSES...

VERSES THAT STOOD OUT TO ME

NOTES

HOW THIS CHAPTER RELATES TO MY LIFE

Genesis

Chapter 26

MY INTERPRETATION OF VERSES...

VERSES THAT STOOD OUT TO ME

NOTES

HOW THIS CHAPTER RELATES TO MY LIFE

Genesis

Chapter 27

MY INTERPRETATION OF VERSES...

VERSES THAT STOOD OUT TO ME

NOTES

HOW THIS CHAPTER RELATES TO MY LIFE

Genesis

Chapter 28

MY INTERPRETATION OF VERSES...

VERSES THAT STOOD OUT TO ME

NOTES

HOW THIS CHAPTER RELATES TO MY LIFE

Genesis

Chapter 29

MY INTERPRETATION OF VERSES...

VERSES THAT STOOD OUT TO ME

NOTES

HOW THIS CHAPTER RELATES TO MY LIFE

Genesis

Chapter 30

MY INTERPRETATION OF VERSES...

VERSES THAT STOOD OUT TO ME

NOTES

HOW THIS CHAPTER RELATES TO MY LIFE

Genesis

Chapter 31

MY INTERPRETATION OF VERSES...

VERSES THAT STOOD OUT TO ME

NOTES

HOW THIS CHAPTER RELATES TO MY LIFE

Genesis

Chapter 32

MY INTERPRETATION OF VERSES...

VERSES THAT STOOD OUT TO ME

NOTES

HOW THIS CHAPTER RELATES TO MY LIFE

Genesis

Chapter 33

MY INTERPRETATION OF VERSES...

VERSES THAT STOOD OUT TO ME

NOTES

HOW THIS CHAPTER RELATES TO MY LIFE

Genesis

Chapter 34

MY INTERPRETATION OF VERSES...

VERSES THAT STOOD OUT TO ME

NOTES

HOW THIS CHAPTER RELATES TO MY LIFE

Genesis

Chapter 35

MY INTERPRETATION OF VERSES...

VERSES THAT STOOD OUT TO ME

NOTES

HOW THIS CHAPTER RELATES TO MY LIFE

Genesis

Chapter 36

MY INTERPRETATION OF VERSES...

VERSES THAT STOOD OUT TO ME

NOTES

HOW THIS CHAPTER RELATES TO MY LIFE

Genesis

Chapter 37

MY INTERPRETATION OF VERSES...

VERSES THAT STOOD OUT TO ME

NOTES

HOW THIS CHAPTER RELATES TO MY LIFE

Genesis

Chapter 38

MY INTERPRETATION OF VERSES...

VERSES THAT STOOD OUT TO ME

NOTES

HOW THIS CHAPTER RELATES TO MY LIFE

Genesis

Chapter 39

MY INTERPRETATION OF VERSES...

VERSES THAT STOOD OUT TO ME

NOTES

HOW THIS CHAPTER RELATES TO MY LIFE

Genesis

Chapter 40

MY INTERPRETATION OF VERSES...

VERSES THAT STOOD OUT TO ME

NOTES

HOW THIS CHAPTER RELATES TO MY LIFE

Genesis

Chapter 41

MY INTERPRETATION OF VERSES...

VERSES THAT STOOD OUT TO ME

NOTES

HOW THIS CHAPTER RELATES TO MY LIFE

Genesis

Chapter 42

MY INTERPRETATION OF VERSES...

VERSES THAT STOOD OUT TO ME

NOTES

HOW THIS CHAPTER RELATES TO MY LIFE

Genesis

Chapter 43

MY INTERPRETATION OF VERSES...

VERSES THAT STOOD OUT TO ME

NOTES

HOW THIS CHAPTER RELATES TO MY LIFE

Genesis

Chapter 44

MY INTERPRETATION OF VERSES...

VERSES THAT STOOD OUT TO ME

NOTES

HOW THIS CHAPTER RELATES TO MY LIFE

Genesis

Chapter 45

MY INTERPRETATION OF VERSES...

VERSES THAT STOOD OUT TO ME

NOTES

HOW THIS CHAPTER RELATES TO MY LIFE

Genesis

Chapter 46

MY INTERPRETATION OF VERSES...

VERSES THAT STOOD OUT TO ME

NOTES

HOW THIS CHAPTER RELATES TO MY LIFE

Genesis

Chapter 47

MY INTERPRETATION OF VERSES...

VERSES THAT STOOD OUT TO ME

NOTES

HOW THIS CHAPTER RELATES TO MY LIFE

Genesis

Chapter 48

MY INTERPRETATION OF VERSES...

VERSES THAT STOOD OUT TO ME

NOTES

HOW THIS CHAPTER RELATES TO MY LIFE

Genesis

Chapter 49

MY INTERPRETATION OF VERSES...

VERSES THAT STOOD OUT TO ME

NOTES

HOW THIS CHAPTER RELATES TO MY LIFE

Genesis

Chapter 50

MY INTERPRETATION OF VERSES...

VERSES THAT STOOD OUT TO ME

NOTES

HOW THIS CHAPTER RELATES TO MY LIFE

Exodus

Chapter 1

MY INTERPRETATION OF VERSES...

VERSES THAT STOOD OUT TO ME

NOTES

HOW THIS CHAPTER RELATES TO MY LIFE

Exodus

Chapter 2

MY INTERPRETATION OF VERSES...

VERSES THAT STOOD OUT TO ME

NOTES

HOW THIS CHAPTER RELATES TO MY LIFE

Exodus

Chapter 3

MY INTERPRETATION OF VERSES...

VERSES THAT STOOD OUT TO ME

NOTES

HOW THIS CHAPTER RELATES TO MY LIFE

Exodus

Chapter 4

MY INTERPRETATION OF VERSES...

VERSES THAT STOOD OUT TO ME

NOTES

HOW THIS CHAPTER RELATES TO MY LIFE

Exodus

Chapter 5

MY INTERPRETATION OF VERSES...

VERSES THAT STOOD OUT TO ME

NOTES

HOW THIS CHAPTER RELATES TO MY LIFE

Exodus

Chapter 6

MY INTERPRETATION OF VERSES...

VERSES THAT STOOD OUT TO ME

NOTES

HOW THIS CHAPTER RELATES TO MY LIFE

Exodus

Chapter 7

MY INTERPRETATION OF VERSES...

VERSES THAT STOOD OUT TO ME

NOTES

HOW THIS CHAPTER RELATES TO MY LIFE

Exodus

Chapter 8

MY INTERPRETATION OF VERSES...

VERSES THAT STOOD OUT TO ME

NOTES

HOW THIS CHAPTER RELATES TO MY LIFE

Exodus

Chapter 9

MY INTERPRETATION OF VERSES...

VERSES THAT STOOD OUT TO ME

NOTES

HOW THIS CHAPTER RELATES TO MY LIFE

Exodus

Chapter 10

MY INTERPRETATION OF VERSES...

VERSES THAT STOOD OUT TO ME

NOTES

HOW THIS CHAPTER RELATES TO MY LIFE

Exodus

Chapter 11

MY INTERPRETATION OF VERSES...

VERSES THAT STOOD OUT TO ME

NOTES

HOW THIS CHAPTER RELATES TO MY LIFE

Exodus

Chapter 12

MY INTERPRETATION OF VERSES...

VERSES THAT STOOD OUT TO ME

NOTES

HOW THIS CHAPTER RELATES TO MY LIFE

Exodus

Chapter 13

MY INTERPRETATION OF VERSES...

VERSES THAT STOOD OUT TO ME

NOTES

HOW THIS CHAPTER RELATES TO MY LIFE

Exodus

Chapter 14

MY INTERPRETATION OF VERSES...

VERSES THAT STOOD OUT TO ME

NOTES

HOW THIS CHAPTER RELATES TO MY LIFE

Exodus

Chapter 15

MY INTERPRETATION OF VERSES...

VERSES THAT STOOD OUT TO ME

NOTES

HOW THIS CHAPTER RELATES TO MY LIFE

Exodus

Chapter 16

MY INTERPRETATION OF VERSES...

VERSES THAT STOOD OUT TO ME

NOTES

HOW THIS CHAPTER RELATES TO MY LIFE

Exodus

Chapter 17

MY INTERPRETATION OF VERSES...

VERSES THAT STOOD OUT TO ME

NOTES

HOW THIS CHAPTER RELATES TO MY LIFE

Exodus

Chapter 18

MY INTERPRETATION OF VERSES...

VERSES THAT STOOD OUT TO ME

NOTES

HOW THIS CHAPTER RELATES TO MY LIFE

Exodus

Chapter 19

MY INTERPRETATION OF VERSES...

VERSES THAT STOOD OUT TO ME

NOTES

HOW THIS CHAPTER RELATES TO MY LIFE

Exodus

Chapter 20

MY INTERPRETATION OF VERSES...

VERSES THAT STOOD OUT TO ME

NOTES

HOW THIS CHAPTER RELATES TO MY LIFE

Exodus

Chapter 21

MY INTERPRETATION OF VERSES...

VERSES THAT STOOD OUT TO ME

NOTES

HOW THIS CHAPTER RELATES TO MY LIFE

Exodus

Chapter 22

MY INTERPRETATION OF VERSES...

VERSES THAT STOOD OUT TO ME

NOTES

HOW THIS CHAPTER RELATES TO MY LIFE

Exodus

Chapter 23

MY INTERPRETATION OF VERSES...

VERSES THAT STOOD OUT TO ME

NOTES

HOW THIS CHAPTER RELATES TO MY LIFE

Exodus

Chapter 24

MY INTERPRETATION OF VERSES...

VERSES THAT STOOD OUT TO ME

NOTES

HOW THIS CHAPTER RELATES TO MY LIFE

Exodus

Chapter 25

MY INTERPRETATION OF VERSES...

VERSES THAT STOOD OUT TO ME

NOTES

HOW THIS CHAPTER RELATES TO MY LIFE

Exodus

Chapter 26

MY INTERPRETATION OF VERSES...

VERSES THAT STOOD OUT TO ME

NOTES

HOW THIS CHAPTER RELATES TO MY LIFE

Exodus

Chapter 27

MY INTERPRETATION OF VERSES...

VERSES THAT STOOD OUT TO ME

NOTES

HOW THIS CHAPTER RELATES TO MY LIFE

Exodus

Chapter 28

MY INTERPRETATION OF VERSES...

VERSES THAT STOOD OUT TO ME

NOTES

HOW THIS CHAPTER RELATES TO MY LIFE

Exodus

Chapter 29

MY INTERPRETATION OF VERSES...

VERSES THAT STOOD OUT TO ME

NOTES

HOW THIS CHAPTER RELATES TO MY LIFE

Exodus

Chapter 30

MY INTERPRETATION OF VERSES...

VERSES THAT STOOD OUT TO ME

NOTES

HOW THIS CHAPTER RELATES TO MY LIFE

Exodus

Chapter 31

MY INTERPRETATION OF VERSES...

VERSES THAT STOOD OUT TO ME

NOTES

HOW THIS CHAPTER RELATES TO MY LIFE

Exodus

Chapter 32

MY INTERPRETATION OF VERSES...

VERSES THAT STOOD OUT TO ME

NOTES

HOW THIS CHAPTER RELATES TO MY LIFE

Exodus

Chapter 33

MY INTERPRETATION OF VERSES...

VERSES THAT STOOD OUT TO ME

NOTES

HOW THIS CHAPTER RELATES TO MY LIFE

Exodus

Chapter 34

MY INTERPRETATION OF VERSES...

VERSES THAT STOOD OUT TO ME

NOTES

HOW THIS CHAPTER RELATES TO MY LIFE

Exodus

Chapter 35

MY INTERPRETATION OF VERSES...

VERSES THAT STOOD OUT TO ME

NOTES

HOW THIS CHAPTER RELATES TO MY LIFE

Exodus

Chapter 36

MY INTERPRETATION OF VERSES...

VERSES THAT STOOD OUT TO ME

HOW THIS CHAPTER RELATES TO MY LIFE

NOTES

Exodus

Chapter 37

MY INTERPRETATION OF VERSES...

VERSES THAT STOOD OUT TO ME

NOTES

HOW THIS CHAPTER RELATES TO MY LIFE

Exodus

Chapter 38

MY INTERPRETATION OF VERSES...

VERSES THAT STOOD OUT TO ME

NOTES

HOW THIS CHAPTER RELATES TO MY LIFE

Exodus

Chapter 39

MY INTERPRETATION OF VERSES...

VERSES THAT STOOD OUT TO ME

NOTES

HOW THIS CHAPTER RELATES TO MY LIFE

Exodus

Chapter 40

MY INTERPRETATION OF VERSES...

VERSES THAT STOOD OUT TO ME

NOTES

HOW THIS CHAPTER RELATES TO MY LIFE

Leviticus

Chapter 1

MY INTERPRETATION OF VERSES...

VERSES THAT STOOD OUT TO ME

NOTES

HOW THIS CHAPTER RELATES TO MY LIFE

Leviticus

Chapter 2

MY INTERPRETATION OF VERSES...

VERSES THAT STOOD OUT TO ME

NOTES

HOW THIS CHAPTER RELATES TO MY LIFE

Leviticus

Chapter 3

MY INTERPRETATION OF VERSES...

VERSES THAT STOOD OUT TO ME

NOTES

HOW THIS CHAPTER RELATES TO MY LIFE

Leviticus

Chapter 4

MY INTERPRETATION OF VERSES...

VERSES THAT STOOD OUT TO ME

NOTES

HOW THIS CHAPTER RELATES TO MY LIFE

Leviticus

Chapter 5

MY INTERPRETATION OF VERSES...

VERSES THAT STOOD OUT TO ME

NOTES

HOW THIS CHAPTER RELATES TO MY LIFE

Leviticus

Chapter 6

MY INTERPRETATION OF VERSES...

VERSES THAT STOOD OUT TO ME

NOTES

HOW THIS CHAPTER RELATES TO MY LIFE

Leviticus

Chapter 7

MY INTERPRETATION OF VERSES...

VERSES THAT STOOD OUT TO ME

NOTES

HOW THIS CHAPTER RELATES TO MY LIFE

Leviticus

Chapter 8

MY INTERPRETATION OF VERSES...

VERSES THAT STOOD OUT TO ME

NOTES

HOW THIS CHAPTER RELATES TO MY LIFE

Leviticus

Chapter 9

MY INTERPRETATION OF VERSES...

VERSES THAT STOOD OUT TO ME

NOTES

HOW THIS CHAPTER RELATES TO MY LIFE

Leviticus

Chapter 10

MY INTERPRETATION OF VERSES...

VERSES THAT STOOD OUT TO ME

NOTES

HOW THIS CHAPTER RELATES TO MY LIFE

Leviticus

Chapter 11

MY INTERPRETATION OF VERSES...

VERSES THAT STOOD OUT TO ME

NOTES

HOW THIS CHAPTER RELATES TO MY LIFE

Leviticus

Chapter 12

MY INTERPRETATION OF VERSES...

VERSES THAT STOOD OUT TO ME

NOTES

HOW THIS CHAPTER RELATES TO MY LIFE

Leviticus

Chapter 13

MY INTERPRETATION OF VERSES...

VERSES THAT STOOD OUT TO ME

NOTES

HOW THIS CHAPTER RELATES TO MY LIFE

Leviticus

Chapter 14

MY INTERPRETATION OF VERSES...

VERSES THAT STOOD OUT TO ME

NOTES

HOW THIS CHAPTER RELATES TO MY LIFE

Leviticus

Chapter 15

MY INTERPRETATION OF VERSES...

VERSES THAT STOOD OUT TO ME

NOTES

HOW THIS CHAPTER RELATES TO MY LIFE

Leviticus

Chapter 16

MY INTERPRETATION OF VERSES...

VERSES THAT STOOD OUT TO ME

NOTES

HOW THIS CHAPTER RELATES TO MY LIFE

Leviticus

Chapter 17

MY INTERPRETATION OF VERSES...

VERSES THAT STOOD OUT TO ME

NOTES

HOW THIS CHAPTER RELATES TO MY LIFE

Leviticus

Chapter 18

MY INTERPRETATION OF VERSES...

VERSES THAT STOOD OUT TO ME

NOTES

HOW THIS CHAPTER RELATES TO MY LIFE

Leviticus

Chapter 19

MY INTERPRETATION OF VERSES...

VERSES THAT STOOD OUT TO ME

NOTES

HOW THIS CHAPTER RELATES TO MY LIFE

Leviticus

Chapter 20

MY INTERPRETATION OF VERSES...

VERSES THAT STOOD OUT TO ME

NOTES

HOW THIS CHAPTER RELATES TO MY LIFE

Leviticus

Chapter 21

MY INTERPRETATION OF VERSES...

VERSES THAT STOOD OUT TO ME

NOTES

HOW THIS CHAPTER RELATES TO MY LIFE

Leviticus

Chapter 22

MY INTERPRETATION OF VERSES...

VERSES THAT STOOD OUT TO ME

NOTES

HOW THIS CHAPTER RELATES TO MY LIFE

Leviticus

Chapter 23

MY INTERPRETATION OF VERSES...

VERSES THAT STOOD OUT TO ME

NOTES

HOW THIS CHAPTER RELATES TO MY LIFE

Leviticus

Chapter 24

MY INTERPRETATION OF VERSES...

VERSES THAT STOOD OUT TO ME

NOTES

HOW THIS CHAPTER RELATES TO MY LIFE

Leviticus

Chapter 25

MY INTERPRETATION OF VERSES...

VERSES THAT STOOD OUT TO ME

NOTES

HOW THIS CHAPTER RELATES TO MY LIFE

Leviticus

Chapter 26

MY INTERPRETATION OF VERSES...

VERSES THAT STOOD OUT TO ME

NOTES

HOW THIS CHAPTER RELATES TO MY LIFE

Leviticus

Chapter 27

MY INTERPRETATION OF VERSES...

VERSES THAT STOOD OUT TO ME

NOTES

HOW THIS CHAPTER RELATES TO MY LIFE

Numbers

Chapter 1

MY INTERPRETATION OF VERSES...

VERSES THAT STOOD OUT TO ME

NOTES

HOW THIS CHAPTER RELATES TO MY LIFE

Numbers

Chapter 2

MY INTERPRETATION OF VERSES...

VERSES THAT STOOD OUT TO ME

NOTES

HOW THIS CHAPTER RELATES TO MY LIFE

Numbers

Chapter 3

MY INTERPRETATION OF VERSES...

VERSES THAT STOOD OUT TO ME

NOTES

HOW THIS CHAPTER RELATES TO MY LIFE

Numbers

Chapter 4

MY INTERPRETATION OF VERSES...

VERSES THAT STOOD OUT TO ME

NOTES

HOW THIS CHAPTER RELATES TO MY LIFE

Numbers

Chapter 5

MY INTERPRETATION OF VERSES...

VERSES THAT STOOD OUT TO ME

NOTES

HOW THIS CHAPTER RELATES TO MY LIFE

Numbers

Chapter 6

MY INTERPRETATION OF VERSES...

VERSES THAT STOOD OUT TO ME

NOTES

HOW THIS CHAPTER RELATES TO MY LIFE

Numbers

Chapter 7

MY INTERPRETATION OF VERSES...

VERSES THAT STOOD OUT TO ME

NOTES

HOW THIS CHAPTER RELATES TO MY LIFE

Numbers

Chapter 8

MY INTERPRETATION OF VERSES...

VERSES THAT STOOD OUT TO ME

NOTES

HOW THIS CHAPTER RELATES TO MY LIFE

Numbers

Chapter 9

MY INTERPRETATION OF VERSES...

VERSES THAT STOOD OUT TO ME

NOTES

HOW THIS CHAPTER RELATES TO MY LIFE

Numbers

Chapter 10

MY INTERPRETATION OF VERSES...

VERSES THAT STOOD OUT TO ME

NOTES

HOW THIS CHAPTER RELATES TO MY LIFE

Numbers

Chapter 11

MY INTERPRETATION OF VERSES...

VERSES THAT STOOD OUT TO ME

NOTES

HOW THIS CHAPTER RELATES TO MY LIFE

Numbers

Chapter 12

MY INTERPRETATION OF VERSES...

VERSES THAT STOOD OUT TO ME

NOTES

HOW THIS CHAPTER RELATES TO MY LIFE

Numbers

Chapter 13

MY INTERPRETATION OF VERSES...

VERSES THAT STOOD OUT TO ME

NOTES

HOW THIS CHAPTER RELATES TO MY LIFE

Numbers

Chapter 14

MY INTERPRETATION OF VERSES...

VERSES THAT STOOD OUT TO ME

NOTES

HOW THIS CHAPTER RELATES TO MY LIFE

Numbers

Chapter 15

MY INTERPRETATION OF VERSES...

VERSES THAT STOOD OUT TO ME

HOW THIS CHAPTER RELATES TO MY LIFE

NOTES

Numbers

Chapter 16

MY INTERPRETATION OF VERSES...

VERSES THAT STOOD OUT TO ME

NOTES

HOW THIS CHAPTER RELATES TO MY LIFE

Numbers

Chapter 17

MY INTERPRETATION OF VERSES...

VERSES THAT STOOD OUT TO ME

NOTES

HOW THIS CHAPTER RELATES TO MY LIFE

Numbers

Chapter 18

MY INTERPRETATION OF VERSES...

VERSES THAT STOOD OUT TO ME

NOTES

HOW THIS CHAPTER RELATES TO MY LIFE

Numbers

Chapter 19

MY INTERPRETATION OF VERSES...

VERSES THAT STOOD OUT TO ME

NOTES

HOW THIS CHAPTER RELATES TO MY LIFE

Numbers

Chapter 20

MY INTERPRETATION OF VERSES...

VERSES THAT STOOD OUT TO ME

NOTES

HOW THIS CHAPTER RELATES TO MY LIFE

Numbers

Chapter 21

MY INTERPRETATION OF VERSES...

VERSES THAT STOOD OUT TO ME

NOTES

HOW THIS CHAPTER RELATES TO MY LIFE

Numbers

Chapter 22

MY INTERPRETATION OF VERSES...

VERSES THAT STOOD OUT TO ME

NOTES

HOW THIS CHAPTER RELATES TO MY LIFE

Numbers

Chapter 23

MY INTERPRETATION OF VERSES...

VERSES THAT STOOD OUT TO ME

NOTES

HOW THIS CHAPTER RELATES TO MY LIFE

Numbers

Chapter 24

MY INTERPRETATION OF VERSES...

VERSES THAT STOOD OUT TO ME

NOTES

HOW THIS CHAPTER RELATES TO MY LIFE

Numbers

Chapter 25

MY INTERPRETATION OF VERSES...

VERSES THAT STOOD OUT TO ME

NOTES

HOW THIS CHAPTER RELATES TO MY LIFE

Numbers

Chapter 26

MY INTERPRETATION OF VERSES...

VERSES THAT STOOD OUT TO ME

NOTES

HOW THIS CHAPTER RELATES TO MY LIFE

Numbers

Chapter 27

MY INTERPRETATION OF VERSES...

VERSES THAT STOOD OUT TO ME

NOTES

HOW THIS CHAPTER RELATES TO MY LIFE

Numbers

Chapter 28

MY INTERPRETATION OF VERSES...

VERSES THAT STOOD OUT TO ME

NOTES

HOW THIS CHAPTER RELATES TO MY LIFE

Numbers

Chapter 29

MY INTERPRETATION OF VERSES...

VERSES THAT STOOD OUT TO ME

NOTES

HOW THIS CHAPTER RELATES TO MY LIFE

Numbers

Chapter 30

MY INTERPRETATION OF VERSES...

VERSES THAT STOOD OUT TO ME

NOTES

HOW THIS CHAPTER RELATES TO MY LIFE

Numbers

Chapter 31

MY INTERPRETATION OF VERSES...

VERSES THAT STOOD OUT TO ME

NOTES

HOW THIS CHAPTER RELATES TO MY LIFE

Numbers

Chapter 32

MY INTERPRETATION OF VERSES...

VERSES THAT STOOD OUT TO ME

NOTES

HOW THIS CHAPTER RELATES TO MY LIFE

Numbers

Chapter 33

MY INTERPRETATION OF VERSES...

VERSES THAT STOOD OUT TO ME

NOTES

HOW THIS CHAPTER RELATES TO MY LIFE

Numbers

Chapter 34

MY INTERPRETATION OF VERSES...

VERSES THAT STOOD OUT TO ME

NOTES

HOW THIS CHAPTER RELATES TO MY LIFE

Numbers

Chapter 35

MY INTERPRETATION OF VERSES...

VERSES THAT STOOD OUT TO ME

NOTES

HOW THIS CHAPTER RELATES TO MY LIFE

Numbers

Chapter 36

MY INTERPRETATION OF VERSES...

VERSES THAT STOOD OUT TO ME

NOTES

HOW THIS CHAPTER RELATES TO MY LIFE

Deuteronomy

Chapter 1

MY INTERPRETATION OF VERSES...

VERSES THAT STOOD OUT TO ME

NOTES

HOW THIS CHAPTER RELATES TO MY LIFE

Deuteronomy

Chapter 2

MY INTERPRETATION OF VERSES...

VERSES THAT STOOD OUT TO ME

NOTES

HOW THIS CHAPTER RELATES TO MY LIFE

Deuteronomy

Chapter 3

MY INTERPRETATION OF VERSES...

VERSES THAT STOOD OUT TO ME

NOTES

HOW THIS CHAPTER RELATES TO MY LIFE

Deuteronomy

Chapter 4

MY INTERPRETATION OF VERSES...

VERSES THAT STOOD OUT TO ME

NOTES

HOW THIS CHAPTER RELATES TO MY LIFE

Deuteronomy

Chapter 5

MY INTERPRETATION OF VERSES...

VERSES THAT STOOD OUT TO ME

NOTES

HOW THIS CHAPTER RELATES TO MY LIFE

Deuteronomy

Chapter 6

MY INTERPRETATION OF VERSES...

VERSES THAT STOOD OUT TO ME

NOTES

HOW THIS CHAPTER RELATES TO MY LIFE

Deuteronomy

Chapter 7

MY INTERPRETATION OF VERSES...

VERSES THAT STOOD OUT TO ME

NOTES

HOW THIS CHAPTER RELATES TO MY LIFE

Deuteronomy

Chapter 8

MY INTERPRETATION OF VERSES...

VERSES THAT STOOD OUT TO ME

NOTES

HOW THIS CHAPTER RELATES TO MY LIFE

Deuteronomy

Chapter 9

MY INTERPRETATION OF VERSES...

VERSES THAT STOOD OUT TO ME

NOTES

HOW THIS CHAPTER RELATES TO MY LIFE

Deuteronomy

Chapter 10

MY INTERPRETATION OF VERSES...

VERSES THAT STOOD OUT TO ME

NOTES

HOW THIS CHAPTER RELATES TO MY LIFE

Deuteronomy

Chapter 11

MY INTERPRETATION OF VERSES...

VERSES THAT STOOD OUT TO ME

NOTES

HOW THIS CHAPTER RELATES TO MY LIFE

Deuteronomy

Chapter 12

MY INTERPRETATION OF VERSES...

VERSES THAT STOOD OUT TO ME

NOTES

HOW THIS CHAPTER RELATES TO MY LIFE

Deuteronomy

Chapter 13

MY INTERPRETATION OF VERSES...

VERSES THAT STOOD OUT TO ME

NOTES

HOW THIS CHAPTER RELATES TO MY LIFE

Deuteronomy

Chapter 14

MY INTERPRETATION OF VERSES...

VERSES THAT STOOD OUT TO ME

NOTES

HOW THIS CHAPTER RELATES TO MY LIFE

Deuteronomy

Chapter 15

MY INTERPRETATION OF VERSES...

VERSES THAT STOOD OUT TO ME

NOTES

HOW THIS CHAPTER RELATES TO MY LIFE

Deuteronomy

Chapter 16

MY INTERPRETATION OF VERSES...

VERSES THAT STOOD OUT TO ME

NOTES

HOW THIS CHAPTER RELATES TO MY LIFE

Deuteronomy

Chapter 17

MY INTERPRETATION OF VERSES...

VERSES THAT STOOD OUT TO ME

NOTES

HOW THIS CHAPTER RELATES TO MY LIFE

Deuteronomy

Chapter 18

MY INTERPRETATION OF VERSES...

VERSES THAT STOOD OUT TO ME

NOTES

HOW THIS CHAPTER RELATES TO MY LIFE

Deuteronomy

Chapter 19

MY INTERPRETATION OF VERSES...

VERSES THAT STOOD OUT TO ME

NOTES

HOW THIS CHAPTER RELATES TO MY LIFE

Deuteronomy

Chapter 20

MY INTERPRETATION OF VERSES...

VERSES THAT STOOD OUT TO ME

NOTES

HOW THIS CHAPTER RELATES TO MY LIFE

Deuteronomy

Chapter 21

MY INTERPRETATION OF VERSES...

VERSES THAT STOOD OUT TO ME

NOTES

HOW THIS CHAPTER RELATES TO MY LIFE

Deuteronomy

Chapter 22

MY INTERPRETATION OF VERSES...

VERSES THAT STOOD OUT TO ME

NOTES

HOW THIS CHAPTER RELATES TO MY LIFE

Deuteronomy

Chapter 23

MY INTERPRETATION OF VERSES...

VERSES THAT STOOD OUT TO ME

NOTES

HOW THIS CHAPTER RELATES TO MY LIFE

Deuteronomy

Chapter 24

MY INTERPRETATION OF VERSES...

VERSES THAT STOOD OUT TO ME

NOTES

HOW THIS CHAPTER RELATES TO MY LIFE

Deuteronomy

Chapter 25

MY INTERPRETATION OF VERSES...

VERSES THAT STOOD OUT TO ME

NOTES

HOW THIS CHAPTER RELATES TO MY LIFE

Deuteronomy

Chapter 26

MY INTERPRETATION OF VERSES...

VERSES THAT STOOD OUT TO ME

NOTES

HOW THIS CHAPTER RELATES TO MY LIFE

Deuteronomy

Chapter 27

MY INTERPRETATION OF VERSES...

VERSES THAT STOOD OUT TO ME

NOTES

HOW THIS CHAPTER RELATES TO MY LIFE

Deuteronomy

Chapter 28

MY INTERPRETATION OF VERSES...

VERSES THAT STOOD OUT TO ME

NOTES

HOW THIS CHAPTER RELATES TO MY LIFE

Deuteronomy

Chapter 29

MY INTERPRETATION OF VERSES...

VERSES THAT STOOD OUT TO ME

NOTES

HOW THIS CHAPTER RELATES TO MY LIFE

Deuteronomy

Chapter 30

MY INTERPRETATION OF VERSES...

VERSES THAT STOOD OUT TO ME

NOTES

HOW THIS CHAPTER RELATES TO MY LIFE

Deuteronomy

Chapter 31

MY INTERPRETATION OF VERSES...

VERSES THAT STOOD OUT TO ME

NOTES

HOW THIS CHAPTER RELATES TO MY LIFE

Deuteronomy

Chapter 32

MY INTERPRETATION OF VERSES...

VERSES THAT STOOD OUT TO ME

NOTES

HOW THIS CHAPTER RELATES TO MY LIFE

Deuteronomy

Chapter 33

MY INTERPRETATION OF VERSES...

VERSES THAT STOOD OUT TO ME

NOTES

HOW THIS CHAPTER RELATES TO MY LIFE

Deuteronomy

Chapter 34

MY INTERPRETATION OF VERSES...

VERSES THAT STOOD OUT TO ME

NOTES

HOW THIS CHAPTER RELATES TO MY LIFE

Made in the USA
Middletown, DE
10 August 2024

58899305R00106